HANDBOOK FOR SINGLE PARENTS

William Rabior, M.S.W., and Vicki Wells Bedard

LIGUORI
PUBLICATIONS

One Liguori Drive
Liguori, Missouri 63057-9999
(314) 464-2500

Imprimi Potest:
William A. Nugent, C.SS.R.
Provincial, St. Louis Province
The Redemptorists

Imprimatur:
Monsignor Maurice F. Byrne
Vice Chancellor, Archdiocese of St. Louis

ISBN 0-89243-313-2
Library of Congress Catalog Card Number: 89-063199

Copyright © 1989, Liguori Publications
Printed in U.S.A.

Table of Contents

Introduction 5

1. New Beginnings 9

2. Pitfalls 13

3. Payoffs 21

4. Parent and Child Relationships 30

5. The Absent Parent 41

6. Parents' Rights 48

7. Children's Rights 58

8. Coping Strategies 67

Conclusion 75

Resources 78

*To our parents
with love
and gratitude.*

Introduction

Jan never wanted to be a single parent. But like so many other single parents in our society today, she had little choice in the matter. Her husband of eight years filed for divorce, leaving her with three small children.

How does she handle the role of being a single parent? She smiled, "Most days I do fairly well, but raising children all by yourself can be a really scary thing."

Jan is not alone either in her role as single parent or in her attitudes. The cataclysmic changes that have characterized our times and have affected virtually every aspect of human life have not left the family untouched. The traditional two-parent family is no longer the norm nor does it dominate the social landscape. The number of single parents is skyrocketing, making it abundantly clear that they are here to stay.

Susan, a single parent for five years, was recently struck by this fact. "The other night I went to a parent-teacher conference at my son's school and everyone in the room, including the teacher himself, was a single parent. It made me realize just how rapidly change has happened."

Statistics tell part of the story. They reveal an evolution/revolution totally unprecedented in the history of the American family.

• Twenty-three percent of the 65.1 million American families are now single-parent families. According to projections made by the federal government, in just a few years one half of our children will live in a one-parent family during some portion of their lives. Eighty-eight percent of these families will be headed by women.

• By the end of this century half of all the children in the public-school system will come from single-parent families. It is abundantly clear that if current trends continue, a majority of people at some time in life will be part of a single-parent family.

If there is a sad side to these statistics, it is that single-parent families represent two fifths of those in poverty, up from about a fifth in 1960. Generally speaking, single-parent families cannot be described as the upwardly mobile segment of our society. Maria, a single parent, knows this all too well.

"If I can paraphrase Dickens, when it comes to being a single parent, it is the best of roles and the worst of roles. I never have enough money, and even with scrimping I just barely get by. Sometimes I feel like I can't take it anymore, and I want to run away from it all. Other times I feel really blessed to have my kids, even if all the responsibility for raising them does fall on my shoulders."

What does the profile of a typical single parent look like?

There is no such thing. A "typical" single parent cannot be found and cannot be easily defined.

Single parents come from every walk of life, race, and culture. They are widows, widowers, divorced and separated, the never-married, and the never-to-be-married. Sometimes a person becomes a single parent by virtue of the fact that the other spouse is absent from home on an extended basis, for example, working in another city, state, or even another country.

We tend to think of single parents as having custody of the children in the family. Sometimes, however, we forget that the noncustodial adult is also a single parent.

From a socioeconomic standpoint single parents are affluent, poor, and everything in between. They are professionals in every field — blue-collar workers as well as the unemployed.

Agewise, single parents run the gamut from the unwed thirteen-year-old girl who has just had a baby to the elderly widowed mother with adult children.

Family therapists across the country are frequently encountering another phenomenon that would appear to fall under the umbrella of single parenting. It is not unusual to find a family where both parents reside in the same home, and yet one of the parents has emotionally abandoned the children. The other is left with virtually all the parenting responsibilities and thus is thrust into the role of "single parent."

Single parents are everywhere and every kind. They are a force to be reckoned with and a social reality that will not go away. Because of the rapid proliferation of their numbers in every sector of society, the attitude that a single-parent family is somehow inferior to a two-parent family has thankfully almost disappeared. There is far more recognition of the fact that single-parent families do not necessarily constitute "broken homes" and the realization that single-parent families can be just as happy and healthy as two-parent families.

"I know that most people would define an 'intact' family as one in which there are two parents, but by golly," said Larry, "I'm the only parent in this family, and we are as intact as any family could be. We are close, loving, and loyal. Nobody can tell me we are not intact."

Churches can be helpful in changing attitudes about single-parent families by reminding Christians that the Holy Family, according to tradition, was just Jesus and Mary for many more years than it was Jesus, Mary, and Joseph. Christ himself was very much aware of the special problems and blessings that come from single-parent families.

This handbook is designed to be supportive of single parents and their families. It is intended to offer both affirmation and assistance to these often courageous women and men who frequently keep their families not just together but functioning beautifully and lovingly at great personal cost and self-sacrifice.

We hope that the insights and suggestions contained herein will benefit in even some small way these single parents who exemplify courage and grace under pressure far more than they are likely to ever know.

1

New Beginnings

No matter how one's *singleness* comes about, it is always a surprise to find oneself not only single but also a parent. A guest on a talk show, recently widowed, summed up his feelings of sudden singlehood with this phrase: "Tag! You're it!"

Elaine, an attractive widow in her early thirties, knows how true that statement is. "When Tom and I decided to marry we were 'going to do things right.' We planned for two years how to have the perfect wedding. We set aside one third of our paychecks every week in a special account; we registered for our china at the proper department stores; we did it all.

"It took over a year to find the 'perfect' dress. We must have gone over the invitation list forty times to make sure no one had been overlooked. The food, the flowers, the gifts for the attendants, the wedding Mass, the trousseau — it was planned down to the last detail. We even planned how many children we would have and when would be the best time to have them.

"Things went pretty much according to order. We were married two years when our first child was born. I quit work to stay home and raise her. Two years later we had a son.

"Then Tom had a sudden heart attack at age thirty. We had five days to 'put things in order.' It's ironic, though, because we covered more ground in those five days than in those two years we spent preparing the perfect wedding. But now it's just the kids and myself, and I'm confused on how to prepare for what lies ahead, except to believe that God will walk with me and will never abandon me, no matter what happens."

Whether single parenthood results from divorce, death, or a choice not to marry, the prospect of raising the children you now live with by yourself, can be overwhelming.

The prospect of "going it alone" is not necessarily negative, as many assume. Even as dysfunctional couples are sometimes able to achieve new levels of health when faced with the responsibility for their own happiness, so too can single parents.

As one social worker observed at a workshop for people starting over single, "Sometimes it takes all we have to just get out of bed in the morning and to keep going from day to day. Much too often we walk around shouldering the heavy burden that comes from 'shoulding' ourselves.

" 'I should have been able to make this marriage work!' 'If I had only lost ten pounds, I'm sure he would have stayed.' 'I should never have taken this new job and uprooted my family.' 'I should have never encouraged her to go back to school. She changed so much!' 'I should have made him quit smoking. I knew it was bad for his health.' 'Why didn't I try harder?'

"The list goes on and on. It seems like there's always something you should have done, and then some magic would have taken place and made everything perfect. But life isn't perfect, and all of us have to come to terms with that sooner or later."

Sometimes, through counseling or association with self-help groups like Alcoholics Anonymous or Adult Children of Alcoholics, a family unit comes to know better family health.

Other times one needs to step back and stop "shoulding" and look at what *I* can do about this situation — to take stock and find out what can be saved and to know when it is time to let go.

That is certainly no easy task. But it is an important one for growth and healing. Like the Serenity Prayer from Alcoholics Anonymous, a person needs to ask God for the serenity "to accept the things I cannot change, the courage to change the things I can, and the wisdom to know the difference."

Martha, a forty-five-year-old divorcee with two children still at home, was faced with rejoining the work force after her husband's departure. "I was so overwhelmed! Someone had always looked after me; and when John left, my whole world turned upside down.

"Then reality hit. My life was different now, and I guess I came to the point of resignation that said, 'okay, this is how it is now. You're all grown up and you're the only one who can take care of yourself.' I think it was then that I knew I was ready to start over."

"I loved Karen and the kids, but even that wasn't enough to stop me from drinking. I blamed her for not making me happy or the kids for pushing me too far. It was all their fault," said Steve, single for four years.

"When she and the kids moved out, I was faced with the fact that I was the problem. At first I thought sobriety would bring them back, and when it didn't I was really thinking of chucking it all. Then one day I realized even if they didn't come back, life was still worth living. That was my first step toward wholeness."

Ted, who is single, recently adopted a young Vietnamese orphan. "It took over three years of exhaustive interviews with an adoption agency before I was approved for adoption. During that time I bought a small home, put some money aside, got all my legal documents in order.

"John was three years old, a beautiful child. I placed him in his new home, presented him with all his new relatives, and paraded his new toys before him. He promptly burst into tears and tried to run outside. That was the beginning of my planned parenthood!"

New beginnings, by choice or by chance, can be a door that opens a person up to growth never thought possible. Surprises come in all shapes and sizes. A person discovers the thrill of being hired for a new job. Another is pleased because the laundry finally turned out right.

Life forces a person to come to terms with who *I* am, all by myself — no longer as the "better" or "worse" half of a couple. For the first time, if I'm doing well or really lousy, *I'm* doing it. And I'm the one to change it if I want to. Now it's *my* turn.

I can be a survivor — first of all as a human being and second as a single parent. I've got what it takes to make it. And with God's help, the help of others, and my own inner strength, I'm going to make my life something very special! Perhaps "surviving" might seem to be a negative idea, like it just happened. To survive as a single parent is positive, forceful, and never easy. It *is* a firm step into the future.

2

Pitfalls

As with any journey undertaken, things always go better if a person knows not only the destination but also where not to travel, and, should a mistake be made, how to get back on track. Single parenthood is a road traveled more today than at any other time in our culture's history. Some of the more predictable pitfalls especially associated with single parenting need to be examined.

"I am so tired, yet I can't sleep. I just want to put my head under the covers and be left alone," said one newly divorced woman. "I'm sad, but I can't cry. I've tried talking to my friends, but I really don't have anything to say to them that they haven't heard a thousand times before. I'm afraid they'll begin to avoid me."

Depression

This new single parent has some of the classic symptoms of depression. Other common symptoms include appetite loss/increase; forgetfulness/absent-mindedness; weeping; headache; digestive problems; high and low energy peaks; inability to experience pleasure; and sometimes a preoccupation with death, including suicidal thinking.

Depression can be caused by a chemical imbalance within the

body, but more often it is the result of a drastic, life-changing event. The death of a spouse or child, divorce, unemployment, birth of a child, new job, and moving are the major sources of stress in our lives.

It should come as no surprise, then, that single parents are usually no strangers to depression. In many cases four of the six major reasons for stress pop up with that first step into single parenthood; they are loss of a spouse, unemployment, job change, and moving.

Whether the relationship that has ended was a positive one or a negative one, the loss of "coupleness" through death, divorce, or separation is extremely painful — one of the most painful forms of bereavement. The stages of grief described by Doctor Elisabeth Kubler-Ross — denial, anger, bargaining, depression, and acceptance — can be present at one and the same time or may be a series of steps taken individually, or even repeatedly, as a person works through the loss of spouse or some other significant person in life.

Anxiety may also accompany depression, the painful emotional feeling that something is wrong or something terrible is about to happen. Single parents commonly report that they are often anxious, that they worry a lot, in fact, too much, especially about their futures and the future of their children.

It is necessary to remember that both anxiety and depression are treatable. If either or both are affecting the ability to function, a doctor or a counselor might need to be consulted. Counseling is usually available through your local community mental health agency, through church agencies, or a private health professional.

Loneliness

Prominent among the most commonly shared experiences of single parents is that of loneliness. Marge, widowed two years and in her fifties, contributed the following: "My friends were exactly the same friends I had before Al died. Some of my married friends tried to be supportive, but they also had obligations to their families. During the day my visits were okay, but some acted awkward if I came over when their husbands were home. Looking back, maybe they were embarrassed that their spouse was living and my husband wasn't.

"Sometimes I almost sensed a jealousy. For example, Tom used to come over and snow blow our walks when Al was alive, but once Al was gone, I could tell that Marilyn wasn't pleased to have him help out.

"After a while I started keeping to myself. I found myself crying over the least little thing. I guess I even became a little paranoid, believing that these friends who had once stood by me now hated to see me coming. I didn't want to put my friends on the spot because of 'poor Marge.'

"I missed Al. He was my best friend. We did everything together. Our kids were great. They wanted me to move in with them. But my life was spent here, in our house. This is where my memories began.

"Dating? That's not been an issue. I've had to go back to work, and usually I am so tired I can't budge at night. Even if someone I liked as a friend asked me out, I think I'd panic. I don't know how to date. I haven't dated since I was sixteen. No, I think I'm better off by myself."

Isolation is one way of coping with the issue of loneliness and avoiding the risk-taking that new relationships bring. Others are so fearful of being alone that they go to any lengths to avoid it.

Jessie, an attractive divorcee in her early thirties, shared her story: "I was afraid to be alone and afraid to date, so I chose an alternate route. I joined everything. There wasn't a night that I was home. I made sure the kids joined everything too so I wouldn't feel guilty about leaving them out.

"One day my daughter Robin said, 'Mom, I'm tired of running away from home all the time! I live at my friends' houses. I want *our* home back!' I realized I had been running away; I just couldn't face the empty house, the reminders of what I had and what I had lost."

Isolation, joining groups, and indiscriminate dating are all coping mechanisms. All humans fear rejection, change, and alienation. "If I'm going to be left out," said Marge, "then I want it to be my choice."

Solutions

What can a person do? Certainly moderation is important. Sometimes it takes a blend of all types of interactions: time alone and with the family, seeking out groups that support you through a difficult period, and forming new relationships, both with women and men. Remember that friends come in both genders.

Also, allow yourself time to "come of age." Adult moral values are established within the individual, not through parental supervision as you knew as a child, but through responsible choice-making. It must be kept in mind that you are a mature adult capable of saying not only "yes" or "no" but also "not yet."

In the case of widowhood or divorce, the source of financial support for many women is ended, and the fears that typically accompany loss of employment are evident, especially for homemakers not in the work force during the child-raising years.

Faced with being "displaced homemakers," they might enter a career-oriented world with little or no working skills or training. Those parents who were part of a two-income family may be faced with decisions to either take on additional employment or attempt to gain more education in order to compete in the job market.

Said Lynn, divorced seven years: "Even with the child support awarded by the court for the care of my children after my husband and I separated, I still worked one full-time and two part-time jobs for three years to make ends meet.

16

"I took advantage of federal funding for displaced homemakers to get a few business school credits and then began working on my associate's degree. I'm forty-seven years old, and I just now have begun work on a bachelor's degree in business administration. I'll be a great-grandmother before I'll be qualified to supervise in my office. It's been hard, but I am stronger than I have ever been. Looking back I am proud how far I've come."

Other single-parent families are not as lucky.

"I had my high-school diploma and two years of experience as a waitress when I got married at twenty," said Judy. "My husband and I believed that it was my place to raise the family, and he would provide for us. Raising five kids meant there just was never enough money left to set aside for a rainy day. Gary died at fifty-four with a mortgage on the house, a son at home, and a daughter in college. I sold the house and moved to an apartment. I finally found a job as a counter attendant at a McDonald's.

"One day, after working two weeks in a row without a day off, I sat down and figured it out. If I had no job, collected food stamps, and lived in subsidized housing, I'd be further ahead. I just sat there and cried."

Recent studies indicate that single-parent families headed by women often see a postdivorce income decline of up to seventy-three percent. Service-related jobs, paying minimum wage, are often the major source of household income for families headed by single women.

In 1983 the median family income for mother-child families was $9,153 compared to $19,950 for father-child families and $28,165 for two-parent families.

The Church today is deeply concerned about such important social issues as feminization of poverty. Many single parents, especially women, have been forced into the ranks of the new poor. All across the country, new programs have been launched to assist poor single-parent families. Services provided include job counseling and networking with organizations or businesses which provide employment.

If you can, try to transform your present job, no matter how insignificant it may seem, into a springboard to something better. That is exactly what Laura did.

"I live in a small town. I was working at a fast-food restaurant among all these kids. Then I began to ask about advancement in the company. I found out there was a managerial training program, and I signed up to be a part of the team.

"In addition, I went to a state career-placement officer and she told me to begin getting a few college credits to enhance my chances of promotion. When an opening came along, I was qualified and moved up to assistant manager. And with that came a salary guarantee and medical insurance.

"Two years later another restaurant chain offered me a manager-ship, and I've been with them ever since. It's not where I thought I'd be ten years ago, but it's not a bad place to be either."

Along with the shock of heading a household alone comes the stress of maintaining a home and job; feeding, clothing, and educating the children; providing supervision or provision of care for young children; keeping ahead of repairs and maintenance; providing medical care…the list goes on and on. What isn't mentioned in the list is quality time for the single parent, time spent enjoying the family and recreation time. Even in the midst of exhaustion can come the nagging feelings of guilt.

Supermom/dad

The "supermom/dad" comic strip character was created with a two-parent household in mind. But what happens to a solitary "supermom/dad"?

If single parents do not experience positive reinforcement from family, community, Church, or one's profession, sometimes the escape route is not only a poor one but actually dangerous, like alcohol or drug abuse, obsessive-compulsive disorders such as overeating, or the development of other negative, unhealthy behavioral patterns.

That is what happened to Jon, a single father of two. "I was so miserable, so tired. It didn't matter what I did, I felt like I was failing. I'd already failed as a husband, and now I was failing as a dad, a provider. I thought if I could just find someone to make me happy it would be better. I didn't realize it then, but I practically abandoned the kids while I hung around bars, picking up any woman who would pay attention to me.

"My mom was handy and I just let her take over. I'd leave the kids with her weeks at a time. Pretty soon I figured I wasn't any good for the kids and that they'd be better off with me out of the picture altogether. It wasn't until my mother said that I was on my own and *I* had to be the one there for the kids that I decided to try and put my life together again."

Sometimes starting over does mean starting from the bottom up. But rebuilding selectively can bring about a fuller, more healthy life than was had in the actual marriage.

For those who tend to control it all — the supermom/dad hero — letting go and letting God may well be the first step toward peace in life. Working, maintaining an adult life, and raising a family are three full-time jobs. Compromises have to be made.

"I was cleaning until eleven at night and would start over again at five-thirty in the morning. I tried to make everything like it was when their dad lived with us. No wonder I was tired," signed Elaine, a divorced mother of three school-age children. Then she laughed, "And not much fun either. One night the kids wouldn't settle down at bedtime, and I walked into their room right in the middle of a pillow fight. Their faces froze as I was smacked in the face.

"I started to yell, and then I threw the pillow back at them, and we had a major pillow war! The room was a shambles, but it was fun! I was as surprised as the kids. It was nice.

"Then and there I rearranged some of my priorities. Sure, when I didn't work the house was cleaner, the laundry caught up, but what I wanted to recapture from our 'other' life was the playfulness and the fun times we used to share. I couldn't do it all — something had to go.

"We struck a bargain — they'd keep up their rooms and take care of the dishwasher, and I'd make sure we had at least one half hour of 'our' time before bed. Now," said Elaine, "the house may not sparkle like it used to, but my kids and I are starting to."

Some other alternatives might be organizing a "kid swap" baby-sitting service with other parents in the neighborhood to allow yourself a night off now and then. Let the kids help you and let them be responsible for household tasks.

If you have close relatives or friends who offer to take the kids awhile, let them. And if they don't offer, ask. Enjoy the time the kids spend with the noncustodial parent — totally guilt-free.

If you can afford it, buy yourself some time: Send out the laundry once in a while or have someone else do the spring cleaning or the yard work. One family saves soda pop cans and uses the proceeds for their vacation. Another woman gives herself a treat now and then by going into a full-service gas station. "Especially when it's raining!" she laughed.

Allowing time to heal — acknowledging that the body and mind need time to deal with all the many changes taking place — is the first step toward reducing the depression and the anxiety which often can come with single parenting.

Letting go, letting God, letting others help, and being yourself are trustworthy road maps that can help you avoid at least some of the pitfalls which can accompany single parenting.

3

Payoffs

"Payoffs for single parents. You've got to be kidding!" Lynn, divorced seven years and having only recently received her associate's degree at age forty-seven, looked incredulous. She paused reflectively, then added, "Let me think about this a moment. I guess I've gotten so used to moaning that I've forgotten about the sighs of relief I have every once in a while when good things happen. And to be honest, they do. In fact, they do quite often."

Despite the minuses of working long hours, a lower standard of living, and going it alone, there can be significant positive points to single parenting. Take the time to recognize and acknowledge them.

Let's rephrase the question: What are the most significant moments in life? When did they occur?

Some commonly shared moments by single parents are those of independence.

"I got home from work and the kids and I sat down and had a 'cereal supper' as we watched TV together. When I was still married I would never have skipped having a hot meal. Joe wouldn't have tolerated it," said Carole, recently divorced from a physically and mentally abusive husband.

Bill is legally separated from his wife. "The first time I stretched out diagonally on the bed, it woke me up. I had all this room, and it felt good. And when I read until one in the morning, I didn't bother anyone."

He chuckled, "Now, don't get me wrong. I didn't mind the sharing when my wife was here. It's just that these little surprises which happen aren't necessarily bad. At first I even felt a bit guilty about taking up the whole bed. But then I realized it's also a new kind of selfishness for me, a good kind."

When partners separate, a new kind of thinking usually begins to take place. "What would you like to do tonight?" becomes "What would I like to do tonight?" Sometimes this is the first time you actually have thought about yourself and what would be in your own best interests.

Lorna, age forty and a widow, recalled what happened to her. "It was probably a year after my husband died, and I was going through the house cleaning out closets. Suddenly I realized I wanted a whole new look in the bedroom. I now have flowers everywhere — the walls, the bedspread, pictures. I love it! I realized that keeping things the same as when Terry was alive wouldn't bring him back, nor would changing things mean I loved him less. I just had to make the house my home now."

Subtle changes take place as healing occurs. Homes often begin to take on the unique characteristics of the new single family. Maybe frills are replaced with tailored items. Deer antlers are carefully packed away and framed pictures take their place. One psychologist remarked: "I watch for these small changes — a new way of dressing, a different hairdo, a comment about a new plant in the home, and I know that healing has begun to take place."

And choices regarding one's spiritual life can start to take place too. It happened to Sandi this way.

"While he was alive, I could not convince my husband that Marriage Encounter was something that we could both find exciting and enriching. After Tom's death I made a Beginning Experience weekend — sort of like a Marriage Encounter with yourself. I wasn't upset that my husband didn't want to share his feelings with me in a special environment — I guess he never was ready for something like that. I just knew that I was ready for a deeper experience for myself. I'm now active in B.E., and I'm happy with how my faith has grown as a result ot it.

"Tom didn't prevent me from personal growth, but I just didn't want to take that step without him. I would have been afraid that he might have felt left out."

There is another side to independence. In dysfunctional families the word "co-dependent" is used to describe the behavior of the coping spouse and/or children, who must sometimes draw upon all their resources just to survive and who often lose a sense of what is normal in family living.

For example, if alcoholism or other addictive behaviors are present in a family, much time and effort are frequently put into how to react to the most routine kinds of situations. Spontaneity is not a hallmark of this kind of family environment. Then when a person finds himself or herself single, greater freedom is suddenly experienced. And this freedom may take some getting used to.

When life has been lived on the defensive, taking positive, assertive steps may require a learning process. There are groups established to help a person not just cope but actually acquire totally new and healthy behaviors. Two of the most helpful with an impressive record of success are Adult Children of Alcoholics (ACOA) and Al-Anon.

I Did It Myself!

Anne's story captures very well how one single parent not only succeeded but actually triumphed. "When Keith moved out it seemed like everything fell apart at once. All the little things I had taken for granted when he was around started looking insurmountable. He was my high-school sweetheart, and we married right after graduation. I had never ever really had to take care of myself. Either Keith or my parents or someone had always been there to look after me.

"Flat tire? No problem, call Keith and he'd figure out a way to get it fixed. Cold weather? Again, Keith would climb the ladder and put up the storm windows. Mice? Keith would get rid of them. Nonflushing toilet, Keith fixed it.

"Suddenly I found myself geographically distanced from my parents, and Keith was no longer here. Sure, there was a phone, but what can your folks do when you are five hundred miles away? After a few tearful conversations, I realized that my parents felt terribly worried about me and also very helpless. So I took a deep breath and started growing up at age thirty-two.

"My first chore: to put up the storm windows. I had waited too long, and it had gotten uncomfortably cold to be outside washing and installing windows! I cried as I climbed the narrow stairs to remove the windows from the garage attic. I cried when I had to put my hand through cobwebs and squirrel droppings to get them down. I cried when the kids handed me the windows as I climbed up the ladder. Afterward I cried as I hugged the kids and we jumped around shouting 'All RIGHT! Are we goo-o-od or what!' "

Sometimes singleness puts us in situations we would not have chosen. But when we face those challenges, we find a strength and inner depth we might otherwise never have experienced.

Anne continued: "My mom and dad came down for a weekend. Dad was prepared to spend his time installing the windows. You should have seen the look on his face as he got out of the car! It was great. And Mom? Well, the admiration in her face said it all. 'I could never have done that in a million years,' she told me. And I knew she meant it.

"Later that night Dad came in and presented me with my own toolbox — right down to extra nails and screws. 'Here you go, Sis,' he said. 'Here is your official handyman, I mean handy*person,* kit. Welcome to the club.' "

Adusting Is Difficult

Often it is assumed that it is just the single woman who has it rough adjusting without a male protector/provider. It's not true. Dan's story underscores that fact.

"After the casseroles from friends and relatives had either run out or dried up, I looked around and thought 'Now what?' My folks had stayed around a couple weeks watching the girls and getting the house resettled while I picked up the pieces following Jeannie's death, and then I went back to work. I had a hot-cooked meal waiting every night. Mom bathed the girls and tucked them in. We had clean clothes and fresh beds.

"The night before they were to return home, Mom called me into the dining room. She had lists and stacks all over the table. 'Dan, we need to discuss where you stand with everything so that you can take over.' I just stood there looking blank. What was she talking about? In one stack were the paid and unpaid bills, with a list of due dates on the calendar. Jeannie had always handled the finances. I would turn my paycheck over to her, and I didn't pay much attention to what happened after that. Now my mom was talking about things like escrowing money for taxes and insurance and making sure to put money in the girls' college fund.

"Another stack was a grocery list of things to keep on hand. 'The cupboard is stocked for now, but you'll have to watch it. As you run out of something, make a note of it. Here are coupons that you can use to save some money.' Coupons! This was unreal!

"After the fifth stack of 'to do' items, we went into the basement and I experienced the laundry challenge. 'Bleach and ammonia can't be mixed; they are lethal together. Colors don't use bleach, prewash grass and grease stains, sort colors and material types.' As I listened, I thought this can't really be happening! But it was, and there was nowhere to hide.

"When they were gone, I thought I would use some shortcuts. We ate out nearly every night. That was my interpretation of introducing variety into our diet. I bought the first thing the kids or I saw when we went shopping. Then I sat down to do the bills, and what a surprise — there wasn't enough money left to pay everything! I had just spent $103 for food, and there wasn't anything in the house to make lunch for the girls.

"When we had used up every clean and semiclean piece of clothing, I knew then I was really on my own.

"I got down the girls' junior chef cookbook and found a recipe for spaghetti. I made a shopping list and bought what I needed. I made the sauce, cooked the spaghetti, and we had some lettuce and bread and butter to round out the meal. 'Dad, this is pretty good,' said Stephanie. Not like Jeannie's, but edible. When the girls and I called Mom to brag a little, I was so proud of myself. That was the real beginning."

An underlying thread to "I did it myself" is the support of the children. Whether it be handing up storm windows to a shaky mom or choking down charred food, the gift of their presence is very important. Invariably, they want to be loyal to and protective of both parents, and so it is crucial to not take advantage of these qualities that they possess.

"At night, when the kids are in bed, I like to go in and just look at them," said Lynn. "Even though they are teenagers, I like to brush back their hair from their faces, plant a kiss, and straighten out their blankets. And just before I leave, I trace the Sign of the Cross on their foreheads — they certainly wouldn't stand still if I gave them a blessing when they were awake!

"I feel they are so vulnerable now, and I want them to be safe. I believe God must look with special tenderness on children. I entrust them to him every single day. I just don't know how I would have been able to keep going if it hadn't been for them."

Dan had a similar point of view. "One day Stephanie said to me, 'It's okay, Dad. I really *like* pink socks and underwear. They all match now!' At that moment I could have squeezed her to pieces! Some days their fighting drives me up the wall, and just when I think I've had all I can take, one or the other will stop for a second and give me a hug. Then I know I am very, very lucky."

Marilyn has been divorced for many years and is now in her early sixties. Her four children are all adults, but she too sees them as priceless gifts.

"The kids would drive up to see me and spend the weekend raking the yard or taking the trash to the dump. They were so supportive. They'd say things like, 'Mom, you're doing just fine, and we are proud of you. Just let us know how we can be of help.' Their patience and understanding kept me going. They loved their dad and me as individuals, not just as a parental unit, and they handled the many changes pretty well. I could never have come this far without knowing they were behind me all the way."

In the shuffle of adjusting to a new way of life, different careers, and demanding educational pursuits, many single parents worry about shortchanging their children. Often, one of their greatest fears is that the children will become casualties of their domestic upheaval.

"I felt so guilty because I couldn't *do* for the kids all the time," Lynn said. "Many times the laundry would back up, and supper wouldn't be started. Then one day I noticed that they had made something to eat and had started the wash just fine. Now we share the shopping duties and take turns putting a meal together. And if I don't call home when I'm going to work late, believe me, I'm in trouble!"

"Although it was always clear in my mind who was parent, I think my children and I exchanged or shared roles occasionally," added Lorna. "For example, when the teenagers were home, they would pick up Nicole, the youngest, from grade school every afternoon. Sometimes Nicki would be watched by the older kids or sometimes by a neighbor.

"One day my youngest teenager went to college; I went about my usual routine. I dropped off Nicole at school on my way to work. Then about four in the afternoon, I realized that I hadn't made any arrangements for her to be picked up after school. In a panic I called the school office.

" 'It's okay, Mrs. Thomas,' the school secretary told me. 'Nicole realized what had happened and stopped in to use the phone. Nicole arranged for someone to pick her up after school and stay with her until you got home from work.' "

Parent forgets child. Perhaps not the best scenario, but what this incident demonstrates is a self-reliance that many two-parent children have not had to develop. Children in single-parent families have half the number of parental staff to wait upon them. Consequently, they are often more likely to learn how to fend for themselves.

Children in single-parent families are also apt to become more sensitive and responsive to adults in their lives. They feel needed because they *are* needed. "I couldn't have made it without you" is something they are likely to hear often from the custodial parent.

It can be frightening to see parents founder, but the lessons such an experience can teach may be far-reaching. Said Lynn, "My kids saw me struggle to make ends meet, to grab pieces of education, to fight for a place in a career-oriented world. Without saying so, I believe it was their strongest motivator for an education. When my oldest daughter married, she did not deviate from her goal of getting a college degree."

Lynn's daughter, Melissa, said: "We saw Mom going through so much. I swore I would never be that vulnerable. I was going to make something of myself, be prepared to take care of myself. Mom was my example. We literally saw her personality grow and bloom, how much pride she had in her independence, and how she relied on her faith that somehow God would provide.

"The first time she made an assertive, positive decision at work, we all cheered. She actually had to learn how to stand up for herself, as well as for us, and it took a lot of courage and conviction.

"When we were being bullied by the big kids, Mom came to our rescue and did as good a job as Dad would have. She was always there for us, pulling for us. I owe her so much."

Often older children from single-parent homes are propelled into the marketplace earlier than their two-parent peers. Finances can't be stretched to cover athletic equipment or to expand teenage wardrobe requirements.

After-school and summer jobs prepare teens for the workplace where one day they will be competing. Recent studies indicate that many children who work during the school year are able to maintain both their grade point averages as well as social adjustments and not lose in either arena, as was previously thought. They learn how to structure their lives and how to prioritize. They also learn to feel good about their accomplishments, not unlike the parent they emulate. Most of the time in single parenting, gifts flow from both the single parent as well as from the child. Singlehood does carry blessings as well as curses. There are always two sides to every reality in life. Still, the old maxim "God never closes a door without opening a window" holds much truth.

Believing in God, believing in children, and learning to believe in self can all contribute to the discovery of just how much good is present in life. In fact, in many single-parent families there is a veritable horn of plenty of God's blessings present if only family members have the eyes to discern them.

Payoffs for single parents and their children are there if only you search carefully. And someday looking back, you are likely to see how far you have come and how much you have grown.

4

Parent and Child Relationships

A single parent is many things to many people, especially to children. He or she is many times the primary breadwinner in the family, not only bringing home the bacon but also the chances are that the whole family stands around waiting for it to be fried! A single parent is the boss, making and enforcing rules, and that rule is the law, at least some of the time.

Such a parent can be a marvelous mother, an excellent father, and many days probably feel like *both* a mother and a father. In reality this dual role desperately requires the addition of major skills.

Todd's mother, Lee, a new single parent, described a scenario with which many single parents will identify.

Todd: "Mom, plea-a-ase come outside and shoot some baskets with me. Tryouts are in two days, and I've gotta practice or I'm not going to make the team!"

Lee, feeling some immediate anxiety: "Aren't any of your friends at home? Can't someone's dad help you out?" She watches Todd's face fall. "Okay, but just for a few minutes. I don't even know how to throw a basketball."

Todd's face visibly brightens: "That's *shoot* a basketball, Mom, and I'll show you."

Lee sighs audibly, and they head outside to the hoop.

Lee realized later that the event had provided her with some valuable insights about her son and herself.

"I really just wanted to crash on the couch and watch the news. I guess I figured Todd has his friends, and his dad picks him up for a weekend once in a while. It didn't occur to me that Todd would want ME to be a part of his life, especially in a role his father had held.

"I mean, I am really no good at sports — not as a child and not now. I don't understand the games. And there I was, Todd moving me this way and that way, bouncing this overgrown ball around. I never even made a basket, but somehow something magical happened between us. I still don't like sports, but every now and then Todd says to 'C'mon,' and we're basketballing once again. I can't figure it out, but it's all right."

What Lee and Todd discovered is that time shared — taking advantage of an opportunity to interact on a child's level — is something very special. Out of habit or lack of interest, many parents can take only passive roles in raising children of the opposite gender.

Men have usually taught boys sports and competitive skills, while women have taught girls feminine qualities and relational skills — an old mode which even in two-parent families is beginning to change. What surprised Lee was that Todd didn't care if she could not give him instructions on the finer points of the game. He just wanted the companionship, a safe arena for attention that didn't involve "mushy" stuff. Mom had become one of the guys, a very high compliment indeed.

Lee knew she was wise to set aside her own biases toward sports and take some risks. For her the risk-taking paid off handsomely in a deeper relationship with her son.

The truth about single parents is that there usually is a void of information concerning the other parent's roles. "Is this how Mom does it? How do you know when it's done?" "Okay, tell me again — I throw the ball with or without a glove on?" Asking questions, seeking advice from children, is an effective way to build their self-esteem, while at the same time building up expertise in parenting skills.

The child has an opportunity to tell the parent exactly how he/she perceives something is done, but more importantly how the child would like to see mom or dad interact with him/her. This opportunity may arise occasionally in a two-parent situation, but it almost always occurs in one-parent families.

Everyone needs to feel important. All of us want to be needed. Often just having our opinion asked gives us a positive sense of self-worth, whether the advice is acted upon or not.

Children frequently have very low self-images. They appear to be insignificant in an adult-sized world. They are likely to think that they know nothing while adults know everything. Not having all the answers can sometimes be the best information a parent can communicate. And if in some instances your child is much better at something than you are, that's all right to accept.

"Gross, Dad. This stuff is just too gross to look at. Here, let me show you how to fry an egg."

Dan laughed. "When Stephanie got her egg done, it looked pretty *gross* too, and we decided on cereal as a safe compromise."

No winners, no losers. Sometimes a pleasant interchange of ideas. Dad isn't too great a cook, and his daughters have some learning to do too.

"I've come to really enjoy our forays in the kitchen. I don't expect I'll ever become a gourmet chef, but the girls think that I have some potential. I just know it's a lot of fun, and above all I enjoy the time spent with them."

Learning together is another form of bonding. Parental wisdom and childhood creativity can be the perfect combination for single-parent families.

Memories created from projects and activities done together will last a lifetime. Be open to the opportunities that arise. Be flexible. Keep a sense of humor. Children grow up much faster than anyone realizes. Before it's too late, go out and do something memorable with your kids.

Discipline:
Necessity, Not an Option

Recently in a family situation comedy on television, a small child was in the process of walking off with her older sibling's make-up. Both children had raised their voices, but the younger child's voice had risen to new heights of high "C."

The father, just waking up from a nap, ordered his older daughter to give the little girl the make-up. "But, Dad, the makeup belongs to *me*," she protested.

"I don't care whose make-up it is!" he exclaimed. "I just want to stop that siren. So give it to her. In fact, give her anything she wants!"

Single parents often want peace at any price. There are no reserves waiting in the wings to come to the rescue; no threats of "Wait until your father gets home!"; no one to say "Did you *hear* what your mother said?" It's easy to get worn down.

Children are very bright, and they read adults with frightening accuracy. After a while it becomes very easy to get into the rut of just saying no. Sometimes the thought of weighing the merits of one more situation, no matter what the problem, is enough to topple the strongest and hardiest of parents.

"There are three of them and just one of me," said Deb, a single mother. "They might be at one another's throats all day, but suddenly one comes up with some crazy idea, and then they band together. I sometimes think the only thing they share in common is how to gang up on me. And it's always when I'm the most burned out.

Lynn and Deb are not unique. Most single parents identify with the same kinds of problems.

Said Dan, "How could I discipline the girls? I mean, they had just lost their mother, and their whole lives had been turned upside down. I gave them a whole lot of leeway and overlooked a lot."

The word "discipline" comes from the root word "disciple," which means "to be a learner." So often we associate discipline with punishment, and yet to teach in the manner that Christ did is an act of love.

Genuine discipline takes the form of sharing your wisdom, your concern and values as a parent, and your insights and experience as an adult. To discipline means to share one's story, one's traditions, with your children — to risk being challenged and questioned as you defend long-held beliefs. To discipline requires a willingness to be open, to listen, to empower children, so that they might take their place as responsible adults.

To bring children safely through the hazards that modern-day life holds requires a consistent message being sent from the parent to the child. Lack of discipline does not just result in children with poor manners or rude behavior. Usually lack of discipline brings about lack of self-discipline in the child, a human being with no self-control and, perhaps, even out of control.

The opposite of discipline is not "spoiling" a child. It is apathy or noninvolvement on the part of the parent. To paraphrase a popular advertising phrase, good discipline takes place "when you care enough to share the very best...yourself."

Interactions between a parent and children may take many different forms, but it is critically important to avoid turning over the parental responsibility of child-raising to the children. Asking for help, calling for time out, acknowledging a mistake, and negotiating are all learning models. But giving up may send two unhealthy messages to the children.

First, they have won. They are now more powerful than the parent, and the parent will do as the children dictate.

Second, forming them just isn't worth the trouble it takes. It's easier to abandon them and concentrate on living your adult life.

Children of all ages have a deep need to respect their parent(s). They may not agree, they may challenge, and most certainly they will push adults to their limit of patience and understanding. Even if it appears that the child has "won" the first round, it is necessary to communicate why the compromise took place.

Said Lynn: "I had gotten to the point that I just consistently said 'no.' It was easier than dealing with more begging, yelling, pleading. I didn't have to defend my answers — end of conversation."

But was it the end of the conversation?

"No," said Lynn. "It was only a postponement until round two. Somehow I thought if I gave in they would walk all over me and I'd never get control back. I was really afraid of losing parental power. It wasn't until I stormed into my room that it became clear we needed some two-way conversation. Ironically, it was the kids who initiated it."

Now what happens when the single parent has given in and given up? Can things turn around again?

Melanie, a widow, went through an emotional hurricane after her husband was killed in a car accident. Two of her three children were injured as well. Melanie was home at the time of the accident.

"I was in shock. Somehow I moved between the funeral home and the hospital until my children were released. Luckily they were not seriously injured. Then guilt set in. I had asked Chet to go to the store because I wanted to take a nap. So he took the kids to get them out of my hair for a while.

"Chet was so great. He took care of everything. When I was at my wit's end, Chet and his crazy humor would take over. I had been an only child, Chet was one of seven. I was the type who went berserk if the pillows weren't fluffed. I don't think he would have noticed if the feathers were all over the couch, let alone if they were 'fluffed.' He was my anchor. He kept me from taking myself too seriously.

"When he died I plunged headlong into severe depression. My mom came and stayed with me for a month or so, but she was needed at home. After she left I went through the motions of getting the kids ready for school and then would go back to bed.

"After a few weeks it became hard for me to leave the house to even shop for groceries. My heart would pound, I would get weepy. I drove at a snail's pace. I was terrified that something would happen if I left the house.

"At first the kids came to me about every little thing, wanting to have me take them places, help with their homework, get them something to drink, an endless litany of requests. I must have somehow begun saying, 'I don't know. Do what you want, just leave me alone.' And after a while they did.

"Their rooms were uninhabitable; my house was as well. Tommy began to practically live at the neighbor's; Susan hid in her room; and only Michael stayed near me, watching television. He didn't even go out to play.

"The kids fought more. Mike, the youngest, would stick up for me, saying that I was tired, and they just didn't care. Susan became angry and sullen. I couldn't tell if she was angry with me or with Chet for dying. And Tommy, the oldest, took over the reins. I would hear them arguing, then they'd run to me with 'Tommy said….' I'd tell them to work it out.

"One day Tommy came into the bedroom and told me we needed groceries. I started to explain I was just too tired, when suddenly he exploded: 'You don't care that Dad died. You don't care about us. You only care about yourself! Why didn't you die instead!'

"I jumped up to slap him, and then I just started to sob. Tommy ran out and I went after him. I tried to reach him and he pulled away. Suddenly he fell into my arms, and we both cried."

Melanie made an appointment with her pastor as a first step toward self-healing. She and the family were referred to a counselor.

The family counseled together and separately. Progress was slow. Tommy and Melanie had exchanged roles, so therapy involved the clarifying and redefining of their relationship with each other. Susan pulled away from the family for a while, but as the months progressed she began to spend more time outside her bedroom.

"It's nearly three years since Chet died. The temptation is to look back and wish it could all be redone. But it can't. None of us are the same people we were when Chet was alive, but we are not any less. Maybe in some ways we're more. There are some things I do rely on the kids for, but I am there for them now too. Easy? No. But it's coming together."

Compromises

What these examples have underscored is the importance of risktaking in the parenting process. The five single parents held on to their beliefs while allowing a new relationship to develop between themselves and their children. Was discipline the most important dynamic that took place? Or was there a sense of give-and-take — negotiation — that was experienced?

The word "compromise" often conjures up an image of someone giving in to a stronger person. For our purpose, however, we will define compromise as the process of listening to both sides of a proposal with the anticipated outcome being favorable to both parties.

Compromising is not about lessening our values but relooking at them from a new perspective. The pat answer — "Because in our family we *always* do it this way, that's why!" — does not promote much interaction. And sometimes there is no time to interact. The maturity level of the parties involved will help to determine what can or cannot be negotiated.

"Raising adolescents isn't easy," said Dan, recalling some past discussions. "Suddenly we went from whether or not they were allowed to cross the street to debates about premarital sex and drinking. I'm not sure any parent is ready for these changes."

Looking at sensitive subjects such as premarital sex often evokes a strong emotional reaction from parents. Many times adults raised in the fifties and sixties were brought up with mixed messages and mixed feelings about their own sexuality.

"Make love, not war!" "Free love!" were slogans heard during those turbulent years. The Church itself was going through a time of upheaval, and unwavering answers relied upon prior to Vatican II now seemed to be matters of conscience.

Years ago drugs were dispensed at the drugstore, not sold on the street corner or in the school parking lot. To "get high" came from climbing a mountain, not mixing chemicals in our systems. So how do you compromise or even deal with these issues as single parents?

Lynn continued to share her story: "I do pride myself for being up-front and open with my kids, and they have always felt it was okay to come to me with anything.

"We discussed all the moral, medical, and spiritual reasons to refrain from premarital intercourse. I stressed the importance of marriage and the need for maturity and a sense of commitment. I thought I had done a wonderful job and was secretly patting myself on the back.

"Then my teenage daughter came to me and said she and her boyfriend felt they were ready for that kind of intimacy. They believed they were old enough — seniors in high school. Somehow I was smart enough to ask for some time to think and to pray.

"We came back together and I explained my position. A sexual relationship implies that a man and a woman are mature enough to take responsibility for their behavior. If the woman were to become pregnant, the male should be able to support the family. There should be stability for the child. And in God's plan for the human race, all these various aspects of an intimate relationship are best fulfilled within the context of committed married love. Did she and her boyfriend feel that they could make that commitment?

" 'No, but there's birth control,' she said.

"I came back to the same question: Can you commit to each other for life right now? Are you ready for the responsibilities of marriage?

" 'No,' was her reply.

"Then until you are ready for that commitment, I expect you to behave in a proper and moral manner.

" 'C'mon, Mom, let's be real here. I'm eighteen and going to college soon!'

"And I surprised myself by saying, 'I understand. But you must understand that there are acceptable intimacies between people who love, and they are not all sexual. I'm not asking you not to love, not to show affection. In fact, I'm not asking you to do anything that I'm not doing. I'm single, I go out. I get lonely too. I am not in a position for that kind of commitment either right now, and I'm asking you — no, us — to hang in there together.' "

Her daughter kept the dialogue open. Heather and the other children knew if they made a decision it would be a conscious one, and that Lynn would listen and not judge. They also knew that their mother wanted them to wait until they were mature enough to handle all the consequences of their decisions.

She made it clear, too, that she respected their values, and when they were adults these kinds of decisions would have to be made on their own. The bottom line for Lynn was very simple: No matter what happened, should a pregnancy occur, abortion would never be an option. In Lynn's home there was no confusion. Was this a compromise? Ask Heather.

"At first I thought Mom was old-fashioned. I challenged her, but she stood firm. Then I also saw that she was very consistent — that she was living out the same principles she was trying to teach us. She knew that I wanted love, but she helped me see there are other ways to express it. My relationship with Kevin underwent some changes, and even though we did not engage in sex we somehow became closer. It was very hard to figure that out!

"I knew that even if I were to decide against her advice, she wouldn't love me less. She would be there, no matter what. Knowing she trusted me and that she treated me as an adult made us closer."

Still another area in which single- and two-parent families are facing compromises is in regard to drinking alcohol. The unbending position of "Absolutely not. Not under any circumstances!" and "I'd better not find out you were ever out drinking!" have had some tragic consequences when teenagers have tried to hide their drinking and have killed others or have been killed.

Many high schools now actively endorse SADD (Students Against Driving Drunk). School personnel work with families to cope with the social and moral implications of drinking. Students AND parents sign a contract stating that if they go out and drink or are with someone who is drunk and driving, they will call the parent/child at home and be picked up. No lectures, no questions. Compromise?

"Yes, I suppose it is," one mother said. "My children have always known I don't want them out partying and drinking while they are with their friends because of all the many dangers. But if it's me holding out and them getting killed because I would not face the reality that they are going to party, I'm going to compromise."

If parents and children can talk together and, more importantly, listen to one another, discipline — teaching, learning, growing — will be equally shared, and the entire family will benefit from it.

5

The Absent Parent

The role of the absent parent, that is, the parent who lives apart from his or her children, is by its very nature a difficult and demanding one. Such a role can be touched by guilt and frustration for a variety of reasons. Tom offered this perspective.

"After my divorce I was forced to move to another state in order to keep my job. I found myself a thousand miles away from my two kids whom I love with all my heart. I was able to see them only a few times a year. I felt like I had neglected them. They felt I had abandoned them and blamed themselves.

"I wanted to see them more often, but it just was not possible. I would call them and send them letters, but a long-distance relationship with your children is something horrible. You can't touch them or see them smile or give them a hug and a kiss. Lots of times when I hung up the telephone, I would break down and cry."

Marty identified with Tom's experience. "I didn't move to another state. After my divorce I lived only a few miles away from my children. But I also had the feeling that by not being there with them daily I was somehow neglecting them.

"I was angry with myself because I couldn't be there when they needed me like I was before my divorce. Believe me, when you don't live under the same roof as your children, inaccessibility becomes a major problem. You have to make special arrangements to see them for the most routine kinds of things, things you took for granted before. And much of the good stuff you miss altogether because you no longer have complete access to your kids.

"My children are now in their early twenties and have a much better understanding of what I had to deal with in trying to remain an important part of their lives. At best it was a very imperfect situation that forced everyone involved to do an awful lot of coping and adapting for a good many years."

The custodial parent often has considerable difficulty adjusting to the role of single parent. What is frequently overlooked or ignored altogether is the fact that the absent parent's struggles to adjust are not easier and, in some ways, may actually be harder. The absent parent straddles a very difficult dilemma.

The absent parent is likely to remain strongly emotionally attached to his or her children without having access to the normal channels of expression for those emotions and feelings. Not infrequently absent parents will turn their anger, guilt, and frustration on themselves. Sally is a typical case.

Sally and her husband, Frank, were divorced after twelve years of marriage. Sally came to realize that she was addicted to both alcohol and prescription drugs, and she made a decision to seek help for herself. Because of this she agreed to let Frank become the custodial parent of their three children. After her successful rehabilitation, she moved to another city and went back to school so that she could forge a career for herself.

Sally's greatest problem to this day is her inability to forgive herself. "I still blame myself for the breakup of the marriage and the fact that the kids are not with me. I know now that I was an alcoholic probably as far back as a senior in high school.

"Frank and I had an amicable divorce. But it was incredibly hard for me, the mother of the family, to give up my children. So even though I made hard decisions that probably saved my life, I still have a difficult time forgiving myself for my addictions, for ruining our marriage, and for putting our children in the situation they are in. In Alcoholics Anonymous I am working hard at self-forgiveness."

Not all absent parents have as dramatic a personal testimony as Sally, but nonetheless they do tend to be unrelentingly harsh with themselves. Parents who are absent from their children can harbor deep-seated anger and self-hatred and engage in harmful, self-punishing behaviors for years — all of which, of course, can take a heavy toll on their happiness and bring about needless emotional suffering and misery.

Sam's problem, however, was not so much his inability to forgive himself as his former wife. For years he refused to forgive her for the breakup of their marriage, which left him a single parent and forced to live away from his children.

He shook his head sadly as he spoke. "I can't believe all the emotional energy I invested in hating her. I even distorted reality and blamed her for things that never happened.

"To make matters worse, I would avoid contact with my kids just to punish her and make her look bad in their eyes. My kids suffered because they really wanted to see me and spend time with me. I suffered, too, but at that point in my life, getting even was more important." He shook his head remorsefully. "What a colossal waste of time and energy!"

Forgiveness, although it is always a difficult action to take, has a special power that enables the absent parent to let go and to move on with his or her life. Forgiveness and freedom go hand in hand, but this truth can only be learned in the doing.

Some Dos
for the Absent Parent

• Do remain involved in your children's lives. Just because you live apart from them does not mean you are not wanted or needed by them. You are the parent, and nothing can ever change that fact. You remain a significant person in their lives.

• Do maintain as much contact as you possibly can with your children. If distance or accessibility is a problem, call or write as often as you can. Above all, try not to forget birthdays, Christmas, and the other special days in their lives.

• Be sensitive and creative. A rose for your daughter when she goes out on her first date or a special note of congratulations when your son makes the honor roll will be appreciated and treasured. Use every means to let the children know that the absent parent cares very much and still wants to be an important part of their lives.

• Do seek your own self-healing and work to rebuild self-esteem and self-worth. If you are having emotional difficulties coping with the role of absent parent, find help. Talk to someone in your Church or to a trained counselor who can guide you through the dark valley of pain, guilt, and anger to new wholeness.

• Do whatever you can to maintain family peace and harmony between yourself and the custodial parent.

• Do fulfill your financial obligations and responsibilities to your children. Payment of child support and maintenance (if necessary) can be crucial to economic well-being and may be instrumental in keeping the family financially stable.

• Do work at strengthening your relationship with your children. In practical terms this will mean making and taking time for them. Good relationships do not just happen either by accident or by a stroke of good luck. Much time and effort need to be invested in your children's lives in order to keep them close to you.

• Do work on communication between yourself and your children. Let them know by what you say and do that they are free to bring anything to you, because you care and you can be trusted.

• Do listen to your children. A famous theologian has said that the first duty of love is to listen. Let your listening be a sign of your love for them.

• Do respect your children and demonstrate that respect in the way you treat them, even when you do not agree with them and they disappoint you and let you down.

• Do try to be as supportive of the other parent as you possibly can.

• Do realize that even though you are the absent parent, you can still be an excellent parent. Make the time you spend with your children quality time, even if the quantity is limited.

• Do accept your limitations. Your family situation is imperfect and flawed, and there is only so much you can do for and with your children. Keep your expectations as realistic as possible or else you will be doomed to a constant sense of frustration.

• Do love your children as deeply as you can and express that love through concrete actions. Make it a point to frequently tell them that you love them, and show your love by what you do.

Some Don'ts
for the Absent Parent

• Don't run away from your role as parent. You may not be with your children, but they still need you as much as you need them.

• Don't engage in guerrilla warfare with the other parent. Feuding and fighting only create a hostile environment that has a definite negative effect upon your children. Children blame themselves for the animosity of the parents toward each other.

• Don't criticize or attack the other parent when your children are with you. Criticism of the custodial parent often puts the children on the defensive and confuses them. Children as a rule do not like to take sides. They want to love both parents and be loyal to both.

• Don't deliberately stay away from your children as a means of getting back at or punishing the custodial parent.

• Don't compete with the other parent for the affection of your children by spending excessive amounts of time with them or money on them.

• Don't allow yourself to be manipulated by your children, and especially do not let them use you to get back at or somehow undermine the authority of the custodial parent. Do not get drawn into power plays between your children and the other parent.

• Don't surrender all the disciplining to the custodial parent. When your children are with you, you have both the right and the duty to discipline them. The discipline of both parents should be appropriate, consistent, and never abusive.

• Don't encourage or allow excessive or unhealthy dependency either upon yourself or the custodial parent. Children need to gradually emancipate themselves from both parents in order to stand alone and build lives of their own.

• Don't feel you have to always approve of what the children do. The fact is that as a parent there will be times when you are bound to be unpopular with your children because of stands you have to take.

• Don't be unreliable when it comes to your children. If you make promises, keep them. If you say you are going to do something, do it. Unreliability can severely strain your relationship with your children and make them reluctant to trust you.

• Don't neglect creating a life for yourself and attending to your own needs. You are entitled to as much happiness as you can find, no matter how difficult your past life may have been.

• Don't be unbearably hard on yourself because you are the absent parent. Constantly blaming and punishing yourself will only make you feel worse and will actually render you less effective as a parent.

• Don't forget to pray for your children daily. Reach out and touch them through the power of prayer. Thank God for the gift of your children and ask him to guide, protect, and bless them. Praying for your children is a beautiful gift you can give to them at any moment in the day.

• Finally, don't despair. Above all, do not label yourself a failure just because you are not the custodial parent. Life is filled with surprises and blessings when we least expect them. For those who let go of their need to control everything and instead let God manage and direct their lives, wonderful things can happen.

As the absent parent, do the best you can and leave the rest to God. With his help, things may work out far better than you ever believed possible. Your life and the lives of your children are still unfolding, and God isn't finished with you yet.

6

Parents' Rights

Single parents have definite rights. The experience of many single parents has repeatedly shown that often they must be strongly assertive in order to remind others, especially the children and other members of the family, that these rights exist and that the single parents fully intend to exercise them. Unfortunately, it is entirely possible, from guilt or fear, for the single parent to give up or deny his or her rights altogether. When this is done, he or she usually ends up paying a high price.

Nadine spoke about what happened to her. "After my divorce it seemed for a time that my life really took a turn for the worse. I was the custodial parent, so I ended up with the children and almost all of the responsibilities. Financially, things were unbearably tight, but worse yet, an unspoken decision seemed to have been made by my children and family members that certain basic rights I had as a human being were suspended now that I was no longer married."

She continued: "For example, when my two children saw me talking to another man, they would get upset and become very manipulative and controlling. Once after I had dinner with a male business associate, my children were so furious that they wouldn't talk to me all the next day. Apparently, in their minds, I had no right to do that. They still saw me as being married to their father, and somehow I was betraying him and them by associating with another man even in the most innocuous ways.

"My mother also started to interfere in my life and actually began to treat me as a child again. When she began to make decisions for me, I knew I had to speak up and confront her behavior.

"I think that single parents, especially women, have to work extra hard in order to remind other people that we are grown adults, fully capable of making our own decisions. We have the right to be independent and to create a life of our own without undue interference from others."

The following are some of the basic rights to which single parents are entitled.

The Right to Relationships
Outside the Family

Single parents usually expend a considerable amount of time nurturing, sustaining, and protecting their families. Sometimes the single parent may slip into the mentality that he or she has no business cultivating relationships outside the family environment. Overprotective children can also discourage them from even trying.

"My children were deathly afraid that I would find a new husband and that they would have to adjust to a stepfather," said Laura with a chuckle. "Somehow I managed to pick up their fears and didn't date at all for the first three years after I became a single parent. Was I lonely? You bet, but in a strange way it made me feel as though I was a good parent, because all my energies went into my family.

"I gave. They took. At the end of the three years I was nearly burned out. That's when I recognized my need for something and someone beyond my family and began to date a wonderful man whom I married. The children had to come to grips with this man, and the whole family is much happier now than we were before."

Single parents do not have to live with the mentality that their state in life has somehow sentenced them to an existence which must be lived out exclusively with their children and other family members with no time off for good behavior. If single parents allow their children to become their wardens, they can count on a lonely existence, especially once the children are grown and gone.

Single parents are entitled to all that goes with having a normal social life. This is likely to include getting out of the home, availing themselves of opportunities to meet and interact with new people, and dating if they choose to do so.

The Right to Privacy

Single parents have the right to a private sector of their lives. This means that not everything has to be shared with the children. In fact, for their emotional well-being it is important that single parents have access to their own time and space, that they deliberately create areas of their lives which are not infringed upon by their children.

Allen, a widower, described his need for privacy this way.

"When I come home from work I try to give my kids as much attention as I can. But they also know that there are times when they have to let me be alone and not intrude. Sometimes I will go to my room and read for a while. Sometimes I call up friends and talk on the telephone for an hour. Sometimes I just want to go for a walk by myself.

Privacy for Joanne means keeping a journal. "I like to sit alone at the end of the day and pour out my deepest thoughts into my journal. For me, journaling is a combination of meditation and therapy that has helped heal some of the hurts which come from being a single parent. Of course, my journal is totally private. Nobody gets to read it except me. It provides me with an area of my life that is exclusively mine and allows me some breathing space apart from the children."

The Right to Change Roles

Single parents have the right to change roles, even if their children and other family members object. Rosemary offered this perspective on role-changing.

"From the time that I was married right up to my divorce, I was a housewife and loved being one. Once I was divorced, however, the financial pressures forced me to take another look at life.

"I was only thirty-five and realized that I might be working for the next thirty years or more, and I didn't want just any old job. What I decided to do was go back to school. I got my nursing degree and now thoroughly enjoy the challenges and rewards that come from being a nurse."

Did her children want her to return to school and start a new career?

"No, they certainly did not!" she answered emphatically. "They knew that money was already tight, and with my return to school there would be even less available for luxuries. That meant if they wanted something extra, they had to get a job and earn the money themselves.

"Also, they had grown used to my being home all the time. That meant home-cooked meals every day and mom available as a chauffeur whenever the need arose. Once I became a student, things changed rapidly.

"The children and I learned some valuable things together during those years when I was switching roles. Our lives are better off now because I did. We have more financial security, and together we are proud of my accomplishments."

For Brenda it was not so much a question of necessity as wanting to change roles. "After my husband died, I had enough money to live comfortably with my children, but I missed being challenged. I went back to school and studied accounting. Now I am a certified public accountant and very proud of myself. I changed roles because I wanted to grow and call forth from myself some new gifts. My sense of self-worth and my self-image have improved greatly because of the decisions I made."

Children may be supportive when a single parent decides to change roles, or they may discourage the change for a variety of reasons. If the single parent is entertaining the idea of a role change, the best approach is honest dialogue with the children. Seek their opinions, offer reassurance, share fears and concerns together, and carefully study and analyze what opportunities the new change may bring to the family. Often a well-planned role change will benefit the family in the long run, but in the short run it may prove painful and demanding as the single parent and children struggle to meet the goal.

If the children are resistant to the role change, the single parent needs to carefully assess how important it is to him or her and how disruptive it will be to the family if he or she pursues the change in the light of disapproval from the children.

If the single parent is convinced it is the right thing to do and has the emotional stamina to weather the wrath of the children, he or she should probably go ahead. The approval of the children may come later, but even if it does not, the gains to the single parent may outweigh the liabilities. All things considered, any role change, for whatever reasons, requires a thorough assessment of risks and rewards and much prayer and careful discernment before it is initiated.

The Right to Have Fun

Single parents are often so preoccupied and busy trying to maintain their families that they forget to have fun. Some single parents even adopt the self-punishing attitude that they have no right to have fun.

"After John died," said Alicia, "I practically felt like it was sinful to have a good time. I remember going to a family wedding and not dancing because I was so afraid of what people might say. Call it survivor's guilt if you want, but it took me nearly a year before I began to relax and enjoy myself again."

Having fun is a good way to allow the child who is within each of us to come out and play. It is a valuable form of emotional release.

Having fun is also an excellent form of stress management. Whether it be joining a bowling league, a bridge club, or a square-dance group, having fun with other adults expands the single parent's social network and enables him or her to make new friends. Having fun with the children can help solidify the relationship between the parents and their children and bring them much closer together.

The Right to Minister to Yourself

Single parents often struggle when it comes to their relationship with God. Not infrequently, for example, when a marriage has broken up, the new single parent will absorb a large amount of guilt and anger and then project both onto the way he or she views God. When this takes place, the God of love can suddenly be transformed into the God of judgment and condemnation. They feel as though he loves them less because of the breakup. Alex was like that.

"When I divorced my wife, I had a nagging feeling that God was blaming me, even though our marriage had been terribly unhappy right from the very beginning, and I stayed as long as I did mostly for the children.

"I didn't go to church at all for a few years, then I happened to bump into my pastor. We talked; I shared some honest feelings, and he suggested among other things that I pursue a Church annulment. I did, and for me it was just what I needed. I learned that God was not waiting to get me just because I ended the marriage. Also I got the wonderful feeling that I was starting over and could actually have another chance at marriage within the Catholic Church."

Many Catholic single parents feel alienated from the Church. Sometimes they are victims of erroneous information. For example, the divorced Catholics may believe they are is no longer entitled to receive the sacraments, so they will stop celebrating Mass and receiving the Eucharist.

A sacramental problem is created *only* after a remarriage without the proper Church annulment. To find out more about the annulment process, what it involves, and how to initiate one, contact your local parish.

Another difficulty when it comes to involvement in the Church is that single parents often feel everything revolves around two-parent families. In a parish setting it is rare to find single parents publicly acknowledged or affirmed.

Often single parents feel as though there is an unspoken attitude in the Church that if there aren't two parents, something must be wrong and we'd better not talk about it.

Single parents need a sense that they are wanted, needed, and respected by the family of God just the way they are. They need to feel welcomed by their parishes, not ignored or overlooked. Far too often, however, this dimension of parish ministry is sadly lacking or woefully inadequate.

It is important that the single parent remain connected to the Church. Prayer, worship, sharing in the sacraments, absorbing the Word of God, can all provide the single parent with much-needed strength and sustenance and facilitate the healing of deep-seated wounds. In addition the single parent should also invest in ministering to himself or herself.

Ministering to yourself means becoming aware of and identifying unique spiritual needs and making/taking time to address them. Fundamentally, too, it means discovering (or rediscovering as the case may be) your relationship with God. Stan described how this unfolded in his life.

"After my divorce I joined an Adult Children of Alcoholics support group. My father was a chronic alcoholic, and I realized that my behavior, including my religious behavior, had long been affected by his behavior.

"My entire spirituality began to change. I adopted the spiritual outlook of the group, which is very much like that of Alcoholics Anonymous. I began to be less manipulative and controlling and started to surrender more and more to God. I used the famous spiritual slogan 'Let go and let God,' and in the process I found more inner peace than I ever thought possible.

"I discovered I don't have to run the universe. God can do that quite well. Above all I discovered that I am not a failure in his eyes, and that even if I do fail, he still loves and accepts me. So I've learned to accept myself, even with all my weaknesses and flaws. For a very long time my image of God was colored by my relationship with my dad. I now have found a spirituality that allows the real God — the living God — to break through to me. All I can say is thanks be to God."

Ministering to yourself is likely to take many and varied forms. It can include spiritual reading, especially from the Scriptures, and perhaps even joining with others for prayer and discussion. It might take the form of a retreat, daily meditation, or praying on a regular basis.

Nothing is more important than our relationship with God. Taking time from your busy schedule to nurture and enrich this relationship means that you acknowledge this great truth and accept it as an important value in your life. We all need God. Single parents need him in particular, because they often feel so isolated and alone in their struggles.

Self-ministry means letting God in so that we can spend time with him. As we get to know him better, we get to know ourselves better, since he has the key to our fullest and most authentic identity.

As a single parent, use any obtainable spiritual tool to minister to yourself and deepen your relationship with God. Try to take advantage of the many rich resources available through your parish church. Above all, do not allow yourself to be driven away from your parish — the "neighborhood Christ," as it has been called — by feelings of guilt, alienation, unworthiness, or indifference. It is your home, and you have every right to be there.

One of the great fruits of every healthy ministry, including self-ministry, is service of others. Take what the parish has to offer but also give of your own self and your gifts in return. Do your best to minister to others and their needs, even if your resources are limited. In the interchange of giving and receiving, you should experience the joy that comes from Christian service and the thrill of growing and maturing in the Lord.

The Right to Happiness

As a single parent you have the right to happiness. Keep in mind, though, that happiness may never be found. It also cannot be purchased at the expense of some other person. Usually happiness comes as a by-product of something else, like loving relationships.

"I have been a widow for forty years," said Betty, her face serene in old age. "I never remarried after my husband died, but I knew I wanted to touch the lives of others, so I began volunteering my services. I read to the blind and spent many hours writing letters for patients in nursing homes and hospitals. I found people in need who were hurting much more than I ever did and who were much lonelier than I ever was. Helping them was my salvation. Without even knowing it, they brought me more happiness than I ever expected or deserved."

Happiness often comes with loving, sharing, giving, and helping, even in the smallest ways. The place to begin looking for it is first in your own home with your own children and then in caring relationships outside the home. And if you are lucky enough to find happiness, don't forget to share it with others.

7

Children's Rights

The single parent has definite rights, but it is equally true to say that the child or children being raised in a single-parent family also possess rights.

"To be honest," commented Jerry, "I sometimes forget about this. I get so preoccupied with all kinds of concerns and with my own needs that I occasionally overlook the fact that my kids have needs and rights just like I do. I think I am a good parent, but I recognize the fact that I have to be more sensitive and tune into those needs and rights more often to make sure they are indeed being met."

The rights of children in a single-parent family include but are not limited to the following.

The Right to Be Loved

The world is full of love-starved adults who never experienced genuine love as children. Children have every right to know that they are loved by their parents. A child cannot be told too much or too often "I love you. I'm so glad you are my daughter (or son)."

Unless children are told by the parent, they will have to guess or try to mind read. And if they are not told that they are loved, they may begin to doubt their lovability. They may think something is inherently wrong with them that makes them unlovable, unwanted, and inadequate. Feelings of not being loved may then impel the child to act out his or her hurt in angry and even bizarre ways. Often it is children who feel unloved who turn to cruel and other bizarre forms of behavior to gain attention.

It is not only crucial to tell the child that he or she is loved but, in addition to saying the words, the single parent needs to use concrete actions.

Appropriate touching is a powerful way to say "I love you." Allowing opportunities for physical contact, that is, kissing and hugging the child, holding or embracing him or her, all give the child the feeling of being loved.

Touching is a form of affection, which strengthens and enriches the bonding between parent and child. Conversely, deprivation of touch is likely to loosen that bonding. Touching the child is another way for the single parent to say, "I not only love you, I like you, and I want to prove it by being close to you."

The Right to Respect

Respect flows from the awareness of the parent that a child is good and a worthwhile human being who deserves to be respected. Children are not clones of their parents. Often they will be very different, with ideas and attitudes which may clash directly with those of the parents.

Respect means that the parent does not squelch the child's right to be an individual but instead acknowledges that each child is special and unique. Respect says to the child: "I think you are a valuable and good person. I will not put you down or humiliate you, even when we disagree."

The Right to Affirmation

Affirmation looks for and identifies what is best in the child and brings the fact to the child's attention by what the parent says and does. The finest kind of affirmation takes place when the single parent underscores the child's very personhood as something good and important even beyond words.

There are numerous ways in which the single parent can affirm a son or daughter. In fact, often the most ordinary events provide the best opportunities for affirmation. For example, the parent can show interest in the child's schoolwork. When grades go up, so should parental affirmation.

"I never demanded all A's on report cards," said Stacey, "but if my children were able to raise their grades by one whole letter, that warranted a trip to McDonald's for the whole family. All got to share in the success of one."

Attending a sports event like a basketball or football game is usually interpreted by the child as a significant act of affirmation. The parent's interest is highly supportive.

"I was raised by a single parent, my mother," said Bill. "She worked two jobs to make ends meet, and yet somehow she found the time to come to softball games and other school events in which I was involved. Let me tell you, you always try a little harder and feel a lot prouder when you know your mom is in the stands cheering for you."

The Right to Healthy Self-esteem

Closely linked to respect and affirmation is healthy self-esteem. Generally speaking, most parents want their children to feel good about themselves. Often, however, they fail to realize and recognize what a critical role they have in the formation of self-esteem.

Positive self-esteem does not come into existence either by accident or a stroke of good fortune. In large part it is formed through a supportive relationship between parent and child in which the parent provides generous amounts of praise, interest, and appropriate feedback.

Appropriate feedback at times can even include critiquing a child's behavior and pointing out areas where she or he has done wrong. This is an ordinary form of discipline. However, what is particularly deadly to a child's self-esteem is an ongoing pattern of negative evaluations.

When this is repeated over a period of time, children usually come to believe that they can do nothing right, and that something is wrong with them. Consequently, their self-esteem and self-image are both likely to be damaged and distorted, and they may spend a lifetime striving to feel adequate as human beings.

When it comes to the development of healthy self-esteem, single parents can provide their children with a valuable assist by teaching them how to respond to failure in their lives.

The wise single parent invites a child to learn from his or her failures, to extract meaning from failure, and if possible even turn failure into something meaningful and useful. In this way the child's self-esteem is not devastated, and the experience of having failed can become an opportunity for growth and better self-understanding.

The Right to a Safe, Secure Environment

Children need to know that their home is a safe and secure place — a haven in which they can count on parental protection. They need to feel that they will not be threatened by hostile forces either from outside or inside the home.

For example, the noncustodial parent should not use the home in which the children reside to pick a fight with the custodial parent. This is tantamount to an invasion that will greatly increase the anxiety level of the children and force them to take sides.

A safe, secure environment means that the children are not subjected to any kind of abuse, whether it be physical, sexual, emotional, or verbal abuse. Some forms of family fighting are therefore totally inappropriate if they involve violence or the excessive use of physical force.

It is, of course, inevitable that the custodial parent and the children will at times have a contentious relationship and will fight and argue. Appropriate expressions of anger can clear the air and then allow the reconciliation process to begin to take place.

This is far different, however, from verbal abuse in which the parent deliberately destroys a child's sense of self-worth through an ongoing barrage of belittling remarks. Verbal and emotional abuse can severely damage a child's mind and spirit. Repairing the damage often takes a lifetime, and in many instances is never done at all.

The Right to Know the Truth
About the Family

Children have the right to know the truth about the family. Every family has secrets, but the children have the right to eventually be told the truth, at least in those areas which are likely to impact their lives. For example, if a child has been adopted, she or he should be told that fact.

When family cover-ups are eventually exposed, children often become extremely angry because they were denied access to the truth. Not knowing family truths can cause children to develop a kind of free-floating sense of shame, a feeling that something is wrong with the family, but they do not deserve to know what that something is.

Determining what should be kept a secret and what should be revealed to the children by the single parent can often be a difficult and delicate act of discernment. In general, the children have a right to know about those things that will affect their overall welfare in the years to come. They should, of course, be told at the proper time, when they possess the intellectual and emotional capacity to grasp the nature of these truths.

The Right to Express
Their Feelings

Children have the right to express their feelings to the single parent, even if those feelings are strong and deep-seated, and perhaps unpleasant for the parent to hear.

"One night my kids and I were having a discussion," Roberta remembered, "and suddenly we were right smack-dab in the middle of what turned out to be the most honest sharing of feelings I've ever experienced with them.

"Believe me, I got pretty uncomfortable when they started to vent their anger toward me and their father for ending our marriage. But I discovered that I was not as thin-skinned as I thought I was. Since then we've had some very honest talks, and we always come away better for them. The kids now know that I am not afraid to listen to them, even when their emotions are pretty raw."

If the single parent creates an atmosphere in which feelings can be expressed without fear, it will go far toward enriching the communication between parent and children and will lead to a healthier and more open relationship.

Understand, however, that accepting a child's honest feelings, ideas, and attitudes and being approving of them are not the same thing. Children are bound to say things with which a parent will disagree. It is the honest exchange of feelings which is good for the family both in the short and long run.

The Right to Love Both Mom and Dad

It is extremely important that the children know it is all right for them to love not only the custodial parent but the absent parent as well. Living with the custodial parent does not mean that feelings for the other parent can or should be turned off by some powerful emotional switch.

The wise single parent will try to create an atmosphere in which love for the other parent is not only accepted but even encouraged. He or she will be sensitive to the child's need to love the absent parent and will not be critical of that love or try to suppress it.

"I remember the first Valentine's Day after Harvey and I were divorced," Tina recalled. "The children came to me and wanted my help with selecting valentines for their dad. For a moment I was overcome by resentment and anger. I didn't want them to share their love with him. He put them through so much that I thought he didn't deserve any of their love.

"Then it hit me that love not shared will die, and I didn't want that to happen to my kids. They will need their father as long as he lives, and they have the right to express their love for him any way they want. What happened? We went shopping for valentines."

If the custodial parent explicitly or implicitly gives a child the message that loving the other parent is not a good thing to do, the child is likely to feel confused and guilty. Loving both mom and dad is something which most children want to be able to do freely and easily, without having to feel that their love is somehow inappropriate behavior.

The Right to Separate From the Parent

No parent owns a child. Parents are merely stewards of their children for a limited time. Children come as gifts from God, and in God's plan these children must eventually begin to separate from their parents and establish for themselves unique identities and lives of their own.

The process of emancipation can be particularly difficult for single parents, who at least in some instances must face the fact that they are likely to be alone. But in order for children to properly develop and mature as individuals, they have to be released to walk their own roads in life.

If the single parent clings to them or tries to hold them back and restrains them from emancipating, the children will experience guilt over the most ordinary efforts at separation and self-determination, such as marrying or moving away from home.

Ruth's story is somewhat typical. "I was left with two children — twins — after my husband died suddenly. I can recall how fearful I became as they moved into adolescence and then closer and closer to adulthood. After all, they were my everything. My whole life revolved around them."

She continued: "After high school they both went off to college, and I honestly thought my heart would break. I went through a grieving process not unlike the one I experienced when my husband died. But then I began to realize that their happiness superseded my selfishness. I know I could not keep them home with me and also have them grow into happy, healthy adults.

"Now they both live in different states, and I see them only once a year or so. We are still very close, but they have created lives of their own and I have mine. Watching them leave the nest was unbearably painful for me, but it was the way things had to be. Sometimes love means letting go."

Growing up and separating from parents is a perfectly normal but often painful process. The single parent can make it easier for his or her children by creating an emotional climate in which children are given permission to develop as unique individuals and are allowed to fashion a truly distinct identity of their own.

By facilitating this, the single parent is preparing the way for the child's maturation and is literally helping him or her grow up. Emancipation is always in the child's best interest, since the formation of a separate self apart from the parent marks the beginning of his or her journey toward the fulfillment of a totally unique destiny, mission, and purpose in life, as well as toward the goal of becoming an emotionally healthy, independent, and capable adult.

8

Coping Strategies

It is important for single parents to realize that in virtually every community there are resources which can be drawn upon and also strategies which can be implemented in the family to make the task of parenting easier. Help exists if only you know where to look, what to ask for, and what you yourself can do.

Anne Marie shared part of her story. "After we divorced I felt a deep sense of panic. The prospect of raising five children by myself seemed overwhelming, and I became very afraid. I could feel myself getting more and more isolated. I felt trapped and controlled by my situation, with no place to run to, nowhere to hide. I think I was getting very close to a nervous breakdown.

"Then a friend invited me to join a support group for single parents in our community. Somehow I summoned the courage to go to meetings, and there I discovered other single parents who had the same kinds of feelings and problems that I did.

"They had formed a support network and were able to inform me about quite a number of resources and services that I was able to use — everything from dependable repairmen to tax experts who prepared my taxes at minimal cost. The group was wonderful and helped me through the most difficult time of my life. I am still a single parent and still attend the group meetings, but now my goal is to be of help to others."

If you are in need of help, support, and friendship, a good place to begin is your church. Find out what programs are available through your local church to see if they might meet some of your needs. Some churches, for example, regularly sponsor support groups of various kinds, including groups designed to help adults cope with grieving, bereavement, or loss.

The local church can also provide the single parent with a free and fairly accessible way to receive counseling on personal issues. Many clergy are trained to do general counseling, or they can refer the single parent to other professionals. Talking to someone who is compassionate and who listens well is often all it takes for a single parent to summon the inner strength to carry on and even resolve major issues in his or her life.

Social services and other mental health organizations, such as community mental health agencies, also offer a wide variety of therapeutic services that can assist the single parent in need of counseling. Usually they are capable of providing individual, family, and group counseling, depending upon what best suits the single parent's needs.

You can locate the names of these agencies in the Yellow Pages of your telephone directory or perhaps by asking other single parents who have been through counseling to discuss the services that proved helpful to them.

Remember: Just because you seek therapy does not mean you are crazy or losing your mind. It is a good sign that you are determined to not just repair but actually rebuild your life and are willing to identify ways to help you feel better about yourself as well as improve your level of functioning.

Whatever you invest in therapy in terms of time and money is well worth it if it facilitates emotional healing and ultimately leads to a better, happier life for yourself and for your children.

If your child appears to have a problem and you think she or he might benefit from talking to someone, start with your school counselor. Often that will be enough to help the situation, but if more therapy seems warranted, you can utilize one of the agencies mentioned above.

Some therapists prefer to treat the entire family instead of just the child, since they see the child's acting out or other unusual behaviors as being related to dynamics taking place within the family system. A few sessions of family therapy frequently work wonders and can alleviate much animosity and anger and help make the family much less dysfunctional.

In many communities classes in parenting skills are offered free of charge on a regular basis. If none are being offered where you live, you might consider forming a parenting group with other single parents. Such a group would provide a forum for the exchange of information, ideas, and effective parenting techniques as well as much-needed support for one another.

Single parents are certainly no strangers to high levels of stress, because of all the demands placed on them. In fact, stress overload is a common occurrence in the lives of most single parents and frequently takes a heavy physical and emotional toll. The more that basic stress management is practiced, the more relief the parent will experience from stress, and its ravages will be less severe.

Perhaps the most important and effective form of stress management is exercise. The exercise of choice preferred by most physicians today is walking. A ten-minute walk has been found to provide more energy than a candy bar and improves one's mood and mental state.

Many psychiatrists now routinely use exercise as a way of treating depression, anxiety, and high levels of anger. Not only does exercise make us feel better, it helps us function better, and it does not have to cost anything except the time to do it.

Eating correctly also helps a family to function better. Good nutrition for yourself and for your children can have some important payoffs. Psychologically, it will make you feel better, lead to better physical health, and enable you to face and handle problems without the many handicaps associated with poor nutrition.

It goes without saying that single parents have to be particularly careful about the trap of alcohol. High alcohol consumption is an extremely poor way to manage stress. Because it is a depressant, alcohol will only make worse the depressed feelings that many single parents experience. It can create both a psychological and physical dependency that will only make the single parent's situation more difficult and actually increase stress levels.

If you feel that you are overly dependent upon alcohol, or if you fear you may have another form of substance abuse, such as a chemical dependency on prescription drugs or illegal drugs, ask for help. You can start with your family physician, contact one of the agencies previously mentioned, or call Alcoholics Anonymous or Narcotics Anonymous. The road to freedom and deliverance from the bondage of substance abuse is often only a telephone call away.

A major source of stress and distress for many single parents is the financial factor. Financial stress is common for most families, but often the single parent feels helpless and overwhelmed by the pressures resulting from "too much month and not enough money."

More effective money management can sometimes reduce those pressures. Again, remember that you need not fight your financial battles all by yourself. Check with your local bank or savings institution to see if financial counseling is available. Often it is free of charge. A professional trained in money management can assist you in important areas like budgeting and debt reduction and help you become less financially vulnerable.

To help reduce family stress, perhaps those involved can form a family council that meets regularly. Talking out problems is a highly effective way to resolve them. Families who talk to one another about important concerns function much better than families who do not talk and simply hope for the best.

An effective family council gives everyone a change to verbalize needs and feelings. Even the youngest children should be made to feel that their opinions and input are valued by the rest.

Family councils that are organized properly and used frequently can lead to much greater family harmony while alleviating areas of tension within the home.

If the council doesn't seem to work well at first, give it a chance and keep meeting until you and the children recognize its value and allow its dynamics to work for you. A family is not a true democracy, so you as the single parent should be the one who has both veto power and the last word in council proceedings.

Another good way to reduce family stress is by playing together. Single parents are often overly serious and tension-filled. Playing is an excellent form of relief and release, a way to forget about your troubles and just have fun.

Playing games and planning activities with your children bring the stress levels plummeting downward and also generate a sense of togetherness. Play tightens family bonds. Games need not be expensive nor complicated. A simple game of softball or playing cards together with your children can have positive effects in a surprisingly short time, and the memories of playing together will last a lifetime.

Still another tool for managing both personal and family stress is laughter. A good sense of humor can rapidly defuse many a family crisis and puncture unhealthy levels of tension. In fact, being able to laugh together is a sure sign of a truly healthy family.

Telling a joke, clipping a comic strip out of the paper, sharing a riddle, are all ways to promote a sense of humor. Humor has an amazing ability to change one's perspective. It can make that which was deadly serious absurb and laughable. It can take the sting out of many of life's hurts.

Recent scientific studies have also found that laughter has a special power to heal and restore both the mind and the body. For all these reasons the single parent is well advised to draw upon humor in trying to create a healthier and more positive family climate.

And don't forget the power of prayer. Prayer is an especially valuable tool in stress management. Those who pray invariably discover this important truth. Prayer invites God into our chaotic lives and helps us deal more effectively with the many problems associated with everyday living.

Prayer can change circumstances, but sometimes even more importantly, it can change us. It can help us cope with difficulties that seemed to be insurmountable before we prayed.

A single parent is likely to discover that prayer combats those two great enemies of the human spirit, helplessness and hopelessness. It can infuse a reason to go on when all a person wants to do is give up.

Unfortunately, when faced with problems, praying is often the last thing we do, as though to say I've tried everything else, what do I have to lose? Try praying first and letting God walk with you through your difficulty. Let your children know that you pray and believe in the power of prayer.

"I believe with all of my heart," said Catherine, "that one of the finest gifts I have given to my three children is the gift of prayer. When they were growing up, we prayed together in church, but we also prayed very naturally and easily at home. Prayer was offered in the morning before every meal and then at night. Why, we would even pause when we heard an ambulance or police siren and pray for those who were in trouble.

"My experience shows that some very important gifts can be passed down within the family from one generation to the next. My children have told me many times how much they value prayer in their own lives, and how they attribute their prayer life to what they experienced in our home. Long after I'm gone they will still be praying. In fact, they'll be praying for me. That makes me very, very happy."

Here are some final reflections on coping strategies. Try to manage your anger or you can count on the fact that it will manage you.

Anger can be a valuable emotion, a powerful tool for self-expression and an energizing force which helps get things done.

Many single parents are not just angry, they are filled with rage; and that rage can not only poison and contaminate the parent's life and the lives of the children, but it can also shorten a person's life span as pent-up hostility takes its deadly toll.

If we allow anger to fester within us, we are placing ourselves in jeopardy in so many ways. Unprocessed anger becomes more and more potent until we lose the ability to control it and it takes over and controls us.

Single parents, like all of us, need to learn how to face their anger, express it directly, and then let it go. A technique for doing this is to simply say to someone who has angered you: "I'm angry. Very angry. And here are the reasons why."

Children tend to imitate what they see in the lives of their parents. If you learn how to successfully manage your own anger, share your success with your children. By teaching them it is all right to be angry but it is not all right to act out that anger in inappropriate ways or nurture the anger so that it is never allowed to be extinguished, you are providing them with an invaluable coping mechanism that they can use all of their lives.

Finally, be gentle with yourself. Try being kinder to yourself — less critical and more accepting of yourself with all your flaws and limitations.

Take as much pressure off yourself as you possibly can. Single parents who bite off more than they can chew sooner or later find themselves staring into the face of burnout. You cannot do everything, so prioritize and do the best you can in those areas that most need your attention. Then chip away at the less important areas a little at a time.

The old saying that often we are our own worst enemy is true. Fortunately, however, we can learn to become a true friend to ourselves.

Befriending yourself as a single parent means growing in self-love and trust. It means being less hostile toward yourself and reducing those negative self-evaluations, which too often are so unrelentingly harsh and merciless and which take such a heavy toll on our sense of self-worth.

Befriending yourself means being willing to forgive yourself when you have failed or done something wrong.

Part of befriending yourself is the willingness to accept and believe honest feedback. For example, if you have done something well or praiseworthy, it is all right to applaud yourself and compliment yourself for the achievement. Use your successes to build yourself up.

If you feel you are a good parent, acknowledge that fact to yourself and others and be very proud of it. Use every opportunity available to enhance your self-esteem and improve your sense of self-worth.

In general, do whatever is supportive for yourself in your role as single parent. All of us have put together a repertoire of coping mechanisms and strategies that tend to be more or less effective at different points in our lives.

Always remember that being a single parent does not have to mean being a solitary parent. There are people ready and willing to help you if you know where to find them and call upon that help. They can share in your struggles and even lift some of the heaviest burdens of parenting from your shoulders.

As you draw upon your own inner strength, with God's help and the help of others you can make it. The road will not always be easy — you've discovered that already — but there may well prove to be much more joy and lasting fulfillment from your role as single parent than you ever believed possible.

Conclusion

Joyce, a single mother, and her daughter, Denise, were talking about a wedding they had just attended. Joyce's three grown sons had been there as well, and during the evening each of the three had danced with her. While they were dancing, each son told Joyce how much he loved her and what a wonderful mother she was.

As Joyce related the story, her tears began to flow freely. "Raising those boys was so difficult for me. They have strong wills and so do I. It seems like we were always clashing. So often I thought I was doing a lousy job as a mother. But to hear them tonight, well, maybe I didn't do so badly after all."

Denise looked surprised. "Mother," she said emotionally, "they were only telling you the truth. How can you doubt yourself so much? You were a terrific mother when we were growing up, and you still are. In fact, you are not just our mother, you're one of our very best friends." Now both were crying, as they hugged and kissed each other.

A tender moment shared between a mother and daughter that sums up what this handbook has attempted to say.

Single parents like Joyce often doubt themselves and may also doubt their parenting skills. They tend to be keenly aware of the clashes, the conflict, and the chaos that go with parenting, and because their performance as a single parent has usually been far less than perfect, they feel ineffective and inadequate. They may even feel as though they have failed their children. Actually, however, the very opposite is likely to be the case.

Without a doubt, single parenting is hard work. It is challenging and at times difficult beyond imagining. But if a parent has done his or her best, then the results many times will be more positive than the parent may perceive.

Stresses and strains on single parents are enormous, but fortunately that is not the whole story. There are also glorious moments of deep joy and triumph that come from not only keeping a family together but also transforming the unit into something beautiful. Many single parents do just that. They take the often unappealing raw clay of family living and sculpt it into a stunning work of art.

Single parents need to be continually reminded of the fact that there is only so much they can do for their children. The goal of parenting in general should not be perfect children but adequate children — children who have been adequately equipped to handle their own lives.

In conclusion, then, we invite you to not be overly hard or harsh with yourself as a single parent. You may not be perfect. In fact, like all of us human beings, you are bound to have your own unique flaws and limitations. Nonetheless, there is still so very much you can teach and offer to your children. In truth you are likely to be the primary teacher of your children in many important areas of their lives. You need not fear that task, because you are probably a much finer teacher than you realize.

There will be times when you feel overloaded and overburdened, when you feel that no one cares, and you are not even certain if you care any longer. At those times be gentle with yourself. Do the best you can and leave the rest to God, whose grace and special strength are always available for the asking. God is on your side. With his help, and drawing upon your own inner strength and the help of others, may you know great fulfillment in your role as single parent.

May you and your children together experience the special joys that can flow from a loving, caring parent-child relationship.

Resources

Education

Community Colleges (Counselor/Office of Financial Aid)
State/Private Colleges and Universities (Counselor/Office of Financial Aid)

(Note: Some universities give credit for life experiences. Inquire at the registrar's office or through adult education.)

State Employment Commissions
Professional Associations (for example, the Professional Women's Club and the American Business Women's Association [ABWA] offer scholarships to women students. Check with the Chamber of Commerce.)
Women's Resource Center (telephone directory)

Job Placement/Career Guidance

Job Employment Services (State Program)
Catholic Charities
Department of Social Services
Women's Resource Center

Housing Assistance

Department of Social Services

Farmers Home Loan (FmHA) (check under U.S. Government in the white pages of the telephone directory or contact a reputable real-estate agent)

HUD (check with county/local Housing Commission)

Shelters (call your local mental health agency or Catholic Charities Division of your diocese)

Personal Guidance

Community Mental Health (look under "Mental Health Services" in the Yellow Pages of the telephone book)

Catholic Charities (through local diocese)

Pastoral Counseling (through your local parish)

Self-help Assistance

Adult Children of Alcoholics (ACOA)

Al-Anon

Alcoholics Anonymous (AA)

Narcotics Anonymous (NA)

Parents Anonymous (PA)

Parents Without Partners (PWP)

Overeaters Anonymous (OA)

Note: For meeting sites and times, check your local telephone directory (white pages), your parish, or the public service listings in your local newspaper.

More Helpful Resources
for Single Parents...

HELPS FOR THE SEPARATED AND DIVORCED
by Medard Laz

Based on the actual experiences of those who have lived through a separation or divorce, this sympathetic book offers hope and guidance to those trying to cope with the resulting sense of failure, guilt, or loss. **$1.95**

HELP FOR WOMEN WITH TOO MUCH TO DO
by Pat King

This book reveals how the author — a mother of ten children — learned to overcome exhaustion, reduce stress, and increase personal satisfaction by restructuring her life. She offers advice on changing lifestyle, outlook, and expectations to meet life with renewed vigor. **$3.95**

INNER CALM
A Christian Answer to Modern Stress
by Dr. Paul DeBlassie III

Focusing on the inner causes that underlie the most common psychological and physical problems, this book reveals how to overcome stress throughout a simple but deep practice of prayer, known as the "Jesus Prayer." **$4.95**

DEALING WITH DEPRESSION
A Whole-person Approach
by Russell M. Abata, C.SS.R., S.T.D., and William Weir, Ed.D.

A sympathetic, sensitive look at a difficult problem, this book helps readers understand depression and its causes and meet social, emotional, physical, and spiritual needs in practical ways. **$4.95**

Order from your local bookstore or write to:
Liguori Publications, Box 060, Liguori, Missouri 63057-9999
*(Please add $1.00 for postage and handling for orders
under $5.00; $1.50 for orders over $5.00.)*